THE
FUTURE
OF YOUR
WEALTH

THE
FUTURE
OF YOUR
WEALTH

How the World Is Changing
and What You Need To Do About It

A Guide for High Net Worth
Individuals and Families

MATTHEW T. SHAFER

CONTENTS

Introduction

I BELIEVE THAT managing wealth has become a daunting task for most people. The world is changing in significant ways that complicate this even further. After almost two decades advising clients, I am convinced of the following:

- Most people need professional advice to be successful.
- Most people question whether they are appropriately managing their wealth.
- Most people can achieve confidence and peace of mind if they take the right steps.

I know that you may have bought this book because you are uncertain about your future. You may have been through some very uncertain times and worry whether you will fulfill your life's dreams. You may simply lack confidence in your ability to manage your wealth as life becomes more complicated. You may simply have a gnawing sense of fear and anxiety about how the world is changing. My goal in writing this book is straightforward. I set out to identify the most important challenges facing successful individuals and their families today and then provide a roadmap for how to address each of them. I have made every effort to explain a number of complex concepts in simple language. At times, what I cover in this book may seem basic; however, each chapter is there for a reason. If you read them all, you will definitely be ready for the future of your wealth.

CHAPTER 1

Why the Successful Have Never Had It So Tough

TODAY IS NOT the easiest time to be wealthy. Maintaining and growing wealth is not as simple as it once was, and wealthy Americans are feeling pressures on many fronts. The ever-expanding IRS code, the volatility of the financial markets, the rising threat of litigation, and the current cultural bias against the "1 percent" make for a challenging climate for successful Americans. At the same time, there are more wealthy people in our country than ever before (over eight million "millionaires"). Of course, being wealthy has always come with a great deal of risk. After all, the more you've accumulated, the more you stand to lose—that's a mathematical fact. But when you consider the complexities of today's challenges, you realize that mistakes are now easier to make. Never before have the wealthy been as exposed to risk as they are today, and managing wealth has never been more complicated.

You may be asking yourself, "Am I part of this group? Am I really 'wealthy'? I'm not considered 'wealthy,' am I?" If you think you are not part of this group, let's get some perspective. The average net worth per capita in 2011 was $69,000. The average net worth for the highest 20 percent income bracket was $292,000. If your income is $250,000 or higher, you are in the highest tax bracket. As of 2011, you are in the top 20 percent if you earn $101,000, the top 10 percent if you earn $143,000 and the top 5 percent if you earn $186,000. Considering these figures, you may actually be (or will actually be) considered more "wealthy" than you thought.

One of the pressures facing wealthy families today is our tax system. The current IRS code tallies in at over seventy-three thousand pages—that's roughly the equivalent of fifty copies of *War and*

Peace. No one person can keep track of every pit-fall or liability that exists in those regulations. If the tax code were simple, if—for example, everyone paid 20 percent of their income and 20 percent of their capital gains, things would be much easier to deal with. Unfortunately—that's not the case; the tax code has never been more complicated than it is today. Because of this increasing complexity, it's very easy to misinterpret tax guidelines or inadvertently do something that violates a regulation. You might make a mistake on your tax filing, only to find out—perhaps several years down the road—that you're being audited or are facing years of penalties and back taxes. I have seen clients who have been working with tax advisors for years and still make mistakes that come back to bite them. If you own any property outside of the U.S., taxes become even more problematic. The bottom line is this: it's easier to screw up. Even if you dot every *i* and cross every *t*, you may be unaware of options available to you that can help increase your deductions, minimize your taxes, and protect your wealth. Have no doubt, our government now monitors every aspect of your finances, regardless of where you go in the world, and the wealthy are often the most closely scrutinized. Mistakes can be devastating and the IRS is not to be toyed with.

Another difficulty for wealthy Americans has been the volatility and uncertainty of the financial markets. I believe we're in a transitional time that comes along perhaps once in a generation—and in certain respects, we're experiencing the kinds of changes that typically only occur every fourth generation. For instance, interest rates have been falling for the past thirty years. This is an environment many people have become used to or simply take for granted. But this trend is now in the process of changing. Ultimately, we're headed for an environment where interest rates will be rising—a new trend that could last for perhaps the next thirty years. Also, debt has been growing in our economy for the past several decades and has reached extreme levels. In the past, debt cycles have reversed themselves, and are likely to do so going forward. This would mean we may be facing a long period in which the economy will no longer be stimulated by growing debt.

The equity markets have been in a similar state of flux and uncertainty. Over the last decade, we've been in what is known as a "structural bear market"—an extended period of lower-than-average returns—and it's still unclear whether this trend has yet come to an end. Unlike the '80s and '90s, which witnessed a steadily and mostly thriving bull market, the 2000s' markets have oscillated back and forth between bull and bear markets every few years, in effect moving sideways over the past fifteen years. This makes investing a tricky endeavor, as the markets are going up and down in short bursts, but not necessarily making much progress over time.

Economies are transitioning on a global scale as well. In one sense, this is a good thing: billions of people across the planet are now connected through technology and digital communication, and capitalism has brought a significant portion of the world population out of poverty for the first time in human history. By 2015, an estimated three billion people around the world will be connected to the Internet. Imagine how many young geniuses and potential entrepreneurs are living in India, China or Africa who now have, for the first time, the chance to connect to the global economy and create something that will benefit the world. Globalization is providing the world economy with the opportunity to harness brainpower that has been, up until now, isolated and inaccessible. The downside to this global revolution is that it makes managing wealth all the more complicated. Markets that were once fairly isolated are becoming fully integrated—meaning that what happens in other countries directly feeds back into what happens here, and vice versa. All of these changes carry with them ramifications for how you allocate and protect your capital.

If you're a wealthy person living in America today, it can often feel as though there were a target on your back. A spirit of envy and class warfare pervades our country and propagates the myth that wealthy people are just "lucky" and don't deserve what they have—after all, nobody feels sorry for the rich. There's an assumption that people who are well off probably obtained their money through dishonest means, or that their wealth was accumulated at the expense of the less fortunate. The cultural media, which broadcasts extreme examples of privilege like the Kardashians or the Hilton sisters—who are "famous for being famous" and didn't earn their wealth (except through reality shows, endorsement deals, and inheritance)—helps reinforce this perception. However, celebrities like these are exceptions to the rule. In my experience with clients, most folks who've accumulated and maintained wealth in this country have done so through years of sacrifice and hard work. They have given up, among other things, time with their families, leisure activities, and the luxury of a low-stress life. They have sacrificed in many ways for many years and put their own capital at risk (both losing and profiting from their entrepreneurial undertakings).

One of the most underestimated dangers to your wealth may be the threat posed by people who want what you have and believe they have a right to it—either through litigation or taxation. It's a well-known fact that high-net-worth individuals are targets for lawsuits. A lot of folks out there are looking to sue people with deep pockets, and there are many opportunities in our justice system to do so (and get a judgment). Many people assume they are fairly immune to these kinds of risks, but there's no telling what can happen in the future—accidents are unexpected by nature. What if you have a home in New England and someone slips on your driveway during an ice storm? Or say your kid hits someone with their car? An unexpected lawsuit could easily result in a financial judgment against you, and you may be forced to shell out monetary restitution to the victim or the victim's family.

In a similar fashion, the current political climate poses risks to your finances. Our nation is under a lot of stress financially, and if our political system decides that certain people can afford to sacrifice even more in order to remedy our debt problem, that's going to put your money at risk. Many

Americans have been less fortunate and have made very little economic progress over the past decade. As a result, these folks are understandably jealous of those who are better off. This all contributes to a climate favoring policies of wealth redistribution.

These tensions also lead to increasing risks with respect to crime. From the economic and sociological studies that I have read, rising income inequality is highly correlated with crime rates (particularly property crimes). Inequality naturally breeds social tensions, which result from feelings of disadvantage and unfairness. At a certain point, people begin to feel more justified in committing property crimes against more advantaged groups. My friends at Risk Control Strategies (a premier security consulting firm) make the point that wealth brings considerable attention and therefore greater security exposures. The wealthier you become, the more sophisticated the criminal you attract (because you are a more profitable target). It is human nature to think "these things only happen to other people"; however, when families become victims of a crime, the emotional and financial impact can be far greater than they ever expected. You might also think, "Well, I am protected. I live in a gated community, I have a security alarm, I stay away from dangerous places." To evaluate your situation, here are some questions to consider: Have you had a security audit conducted by a competent specialist (beyond the alarm company)? Do you have encryption for your wireless network? Have you completed background checks on everyone who works in your home? Have you trained your family about the risks of social media and social networks? Do you use a professional service to safeguard against identity theft? If you answered no (or I don't know) to any of these questions, then you may be exposed.

So what can you do to protect yourself from all these risks? Sometimes it might seem like the best thing to do would be to pull out and run for cover. During my meetings with clients, I often get this question: "What if we just wanted to stop and not lose anything? What could we do?" Unfortunately, this isn't an option. Sure, if you have a few thousand dollars, you can put it in an FDIC-insured bank and you'll be backed up pretty well. But once you accumulate a certain amount of wealth, there's nowhere in the world you can park that money so that it's completely insulated from risk. Even if you sold everything and locked up your cash in a bunker, it would still be exposed to inflation. Inflation rates are low right now but could easily move higher. Yet even at 3 percent inflation, your money will lose half its value in twenty-four years. You can never really hide out or completely isolate your wealth from risk, as appealing as this might seem during these tumultuous times. That's one of the burdens that come with wealth in this day and age: You're responsible for a lot—and there's a lot that can go wrong.

Perhaps you're reading this and thinking, "Doesn't my wealth insulate me from all these things? Aren't I above it all?" Perhaps you've considered these risks but don't quite understand how these issues affect you personally. What does it all mean to your own bottom line, your own peace of mind, your own sense of security for you and your family? You may just have a general sense of fear or concern, or you may be acutely aware of these challenges in great detail but are just not sure what to do. That's what I hope to show you in this book. The truth is everybody is exposed to risk. That's why families, today more than ever, need a team of advisors who understand these threats and can be forward-looking in how to mitigate those risks. Wealthy families cannot do this work themselves— especially if they want to have time to enjoy their wealth, focus on work, run their businesses and spend time with their families. They need a team of advisors who are aware of all these issues and diligently seek out new solutions to best navigate this environment. In this way, competent advisors can help you do all that is possible to reduce and diversify away these risks, so that no single misfortune can wipe you out.

CHAPTER 2

Manage Your Wealth, Not Just Your Assets

MOST FINANCIAL ADVISORS today focus their energy on managing their clients' liquid assets—building portfolios of stocks and bonds and managing other financial securities. The truth is that these kinds of investments often comprise only a portion of your overall wealth. Many financial advisors claim to manage wealth in a comprehensive way, when in reality they are mostly managing investible assets. To truly protect and optimize your finances, you need to manage your total wealth in a synchronized fashion.

Beyond your investment portfolio, what constitutes wealth? Think about the businesses you've built from the ground up, or your family's real estate portfolio. Consider your vacation homes and other properties. There are also the less-tangible forms of wealth—assets that are more difficult to measure in financial terms such as your legacy, your children and the human capital that exists in your family. It includes your health and wellbeing. Wealth management takes into account all of these factors, not just the part that exists in the brokerage account. Understanding the "whole picture" of your family's wealth is the foundation to protecting your assets from potential threats. What exposures do you have to litigation and taxation? Are there any gaps in your insurance policies? What else could jeopardize your finances? Wealth management goes beyond simply managing assets and includes proactively insulating them from risks—often through working closely with other advisors and specialists. Effective wealth management is a collaborative effort. It involves a team of professionals working together—from attorneys and insurance agents to security specialists and accounting professionals. It means bringing in and engaging with specialists (when needed) to address your specific concerns. It could even involve connecting you with experts who can help you talk to your children about wealth, so that the next generation can become good stewards of the family legacy.

People often ask me to describe the typical client we work with. While we don't work exclusively with a specific industry sector or geographical area—such as doctors in California or lawyers in Boston—we have found that the clients who benefit the most from our services typically share several common traits:

- They value the simplicity and freedom that come from delegating financial matters to a competent, trustworthy, and experienced advisory team.
- They are passionate about their desire to accomplish their goals and realize that achieving those goals requires planning, a long-term perspective, and strategic thinking.

- They value an integrated approach involving all aspects of holistic wealth management.
- They are people who have accumulated enough wealth that they are now experiencing some of the complexities that accompany that wealth.
- They value spending time on other things that are truly important to them.

In other words, these are families who are building, or have already built their wealth and are interested in preserving it in a way that will ultimately simplify their lives and enhance their ability to enjoy what they've earned. If they've already hit a home run—now they don't want to strike out. These tend to be families who accumulate wealth through a private business, real estate, or a career in a highly compensated profession.

Who don't we serve? Well, we don't typically work well with people who are looking to get rich quick, or folks who are just after hot investment ideas and have no desire to coordinate the other aspects of their lives into a comprehensive wealth management system. People like this tend not to delegate to other professionals—they want to do everything themselves, keeping their advisors isolated from one another, so that they can dictate the details of how things get done. We value a synchronized approach to wealth management, and we can't accomplish the best outcomes for clients if we're not able to see the whole picture.

I recently had prospective clients who'd heard about me via an article I had written come into my office. They had several million dollars at a private bank, and seemed very eager to meet. When I asked what brought them in to see me, they said, "We don't believe our portfolio results are what they should be."

"Interesting," I said. "Do you know why? Is your advisor not communicating to you what's happening?"

"No, no," they said. "That's all fine. Our advisor keeps us up to date."

"Are you not properly diversified?" I asked.

They told me that wasn't the issue either. "What we want is someone who's going to make us more money. We want an advisor who is going to get us more returns when there's an opportunity, and then get us out of risk before the markets start going down. We want to know: how do you do that?"

The truth is nobody can achieve such perfect results. I could have made empty promises and told them I had the silver-bullet solution to always making money and never losing any, but that would have been very disappointing for them when those promises did not actually materialize. I tried to dig deeper, asking them about their estate plans, any real estate they owned, their businesses, but they didn't want to have a more meaningful discussion.

In the end, I let them know that we probably weren't a good fit for them. I explained that our process is more holistic in nature. "This is how we can add more value," I said. "However, I know some other folks who specialize in trying to accomplish what you are looking for. I'd be happy to connect you with them. But keep your expectations realistic—I have never found an investment process as perfect as the one you are looking for." Having these forthright conversations upfront helps set the proper expectations. I've found that a key to creating lasting relationships and garnering trust is to be honest about what I can do for clients, and what is simply not possible.

Health Is Wealth

Health is an aspect of wealth management that many financial advisors overlook, and it's an area that is becoming more complicated. The Affordable Care Act is going to dramatically overhaul the process of accessing quality healthcare, because it further complicates the doctor–patient relationship. The best doctors may soon migrate to a model where they are paid directly by their patients, without the middleman of the insurance company or Medicare. Essentially, many wealthy people may end up choosing to pay out of pocket for concierge medical services. Decisions about your health are likely going to become more involved and complex as this legislation goes into effect. Your health is an invaluable component of your total worth, and it's more important than ever to have a financial advisor who will help guide you through this new and challenging landscape.

If you own a business, the Affordable Care Act could dramatically impact your whole profit model. The law mandates that business owners provide certain insurance options to their full-time employees or incur a fine. This means that business owners may be facing substantially higher costs one way or another.

A Team Needs a Quarterback

Like I said, most financial advisors focus on asset management. They help clients make investment decisions, but they spend little time engaging in other areas of a client's life. Often, this is because advisors simply don't possess the skill set necessary to navigate these other aspects of wealth. Sometimes, advisors are just not comfortable or confident having conversations about these complicated sub-jects. Advisors may even avoid making the effort because they are not directly compensated for this work. Either way, an advisor must devote a lot of time to learn enough about these other disciplines so that he or she can effectively collaborate with the other professionals who work for your family. Elite advisors must continually educate themselves regarding the best and latest practices to effectively protect and grow their clients' financial, physical and human capital.

I consider myself fortunate that I learned the importance of this holistic approach early in my career. It started out as simple curiosity—a desire to understand how things fit together. Rather than sticking to the traditional financial advisor model—questioning clients about their preference for growth or income, or asking whether they are aggressive, moderate or conservative—I would try to get a more well-rounded understanding of their lives and what they truly value. For example, if my client owned a business, I would ask, "How did you build it? What are your plans for it? How are your kids involved in it?" One of my favorite questions is, "In a perfect world, what would your future look like?" In doing this, I realized that there were areas of my clients' lives that were just as important as their investment accounts.

I'm a problem solver by nature—the kind of person who enjoys analyzing situations, building solutions, and putting the whole picture together. I realized that I couldn't have a meaningful impact on a family's total wealth unless I spoke with them about those other aspects of wealth that were often more important than their brokerage account. It also occurred to me that years of successful investing could be obliterated by a number of unforeseen risks (from outside the investment portfolio). This motivated me to learn more about the other disciplines that are involved in managing wealth. I sought out training and guidance from experts in these fields, and I've spent almost two decades now fine-tuning these skills.

As I mentioned, an important component of

effective wealth management is coordination of advice. If a family's assets are managed by separate advisors who have little communication with one another, their strategies will not be coordinated. And if things are not coordinated, the results will not be optimized. Within your circle of advisors, you need someone to synchronize things. Likewise, you need someone who will provide a central point of access to outside experts when they are needed. Who better to do this job than your financial advisor? Financial advisors have the occasion to talk to their clients more frequently than does the accountant, the lawyer, the insurance agent, or the family physician. A good financial advisor should be able to quarterback your total wealth, to work in harmony with your other advisors using that "big picture" knowledge to actively identify potential problems and seek out solutions ahead of time.

We have built a team of vetted professionals in many disciplines, and we know whom to bring in and when. Here are some examples of the professionals we work with:

- A network of highly competent attorneys specializing in estate planning, asset protection, real estate, business succession, special needs, and various kinds of litigation.
- A network of accounting and tax specialists.
- A network of insurance specialists to provide comprehensive, coordinated, and cost-effective coverage.
- A network of bankers to provide lending, corporate, and investment banking services.
- Planning specialists who can help with things like philanthropy and family governance.
- Retirement-plan administrators.
- Security consultants.

While not every client needs each of these services, we are able to help our clients readily access this network when needed.

Wealth Management in Action

To illustrate how comprehensive wealth management works in practice, I'll share with you the story of a client I began working with several years ago—a man I'll call Jim. Jim was a business owner who had more than half his net worth in a family-run company. Part of my discovery process—as I mentioned before—involves talking one-on-one with clients about their businesses, their plans, and their vision for the future. It was during one of these discussions that Jim revealed to me his concerns about the future of his business. He planned to retire in a few years, but had no idea what would happen to his business if he did. His children didn't work for the company and had no interest in doing so. Jim had no succession plan and had done very little to prepare for this eventual transition.

I convinced Jim that now was the time to start considering exit strategies and forming a plan. Because retirement was still a few years down the road, there was time for such planning to make a real difference. The first step was looking at his tax situation and the future of his estate. We met with his other advisors to review how the business was currently owned and consider future tax issues such as capital gains and estate taxes. Through these meetings, we were able to structure some gifting of company shares to the kids at discounted values to leverage the use of Jim's estate and gift exclusions.

I also brought in a business analyst that specialized in Jim's industry. This analyst worked with Jim to prepare his company for future sale, taking steps to make the business more attractive to potential buyers and preparing the management staff to continue running the business successfully after Jim's departure.

A year before Jim planned to retire, I helped him work with his advisors to model and analyze several sale alternatives: A financial purchase by a private equity firm? An outright sale to a strategic buyer? A sale to an employee stock ownership plan? After carefully going over the pros and cons of each option, Jim decided to pursue a combination of the latter two: the employee stock ownership plan would function as a backup option, in case a buyer could not be found. Over the next several months, we brought in an investment-banking expert who secured several offers from strategic buyers. However, Jim ultimately decided to sell to an employee stock ownership plan—and he was glad he already had the planning in place to do so.

Because of the work we did preparing Jim for this transition, we were able to structure the sale so that the capital gains taxes on the proceeds were deferred for the rest of his life—and would be for good, upon his death. Using some additional techniques, we were able to arrange things so that additional proceeds of the business sale were transferred to Jim's children and grandchildren with minimal estate or gift taxes. This preparation and planning resulted in millions of extra after-tax wealth for the family, and gave Jim the peace of mind to truly enjoy his retirement.

Life transitions—such as retirement—can present a number of potential risks to your wealth, all of which require expert planning and proactive coordination with other specialists. But even during times of relative stability, your wealth can be at risk in other ways—through oversights, lack of coordination, or simple human error.

I'll also share with you the story of a client I'll call Paul. Paul's family had a large collection of assets spread across the country—multiple properties, businesses, and vehicles in multiple states. The family had set up a number of trusts and partnerships, which they believed shielded their assets from many potential risks. However, as I began to review these assets, I found that many of them were not titled to match the estate planning he had put in place. In the event of a lawsuit, the family would be exposed to millions of dollars of potential loses.

Making sure these assets were protected involved reaching out to the family's other experts and advisors. The first person I got in touch with was the family's tax and legal advisors. Together with the family, we made sure that these assets were properly titled in such a way that would help protect Paul and his family from these types of financial hazards.

The next step was bringing in an insurance specialist to review the family's coverage. Upon reviewing the properties and businesses, we discovered that several policies had been put in place that did not match the title and entity owner of the properties. This was a potential nightmare: in the event of a claim, the insurance company could deny payment because of these errors. We also discovered that a number of policies had significant liability gaps. Through working with the insurance specialist, we were able to coordinate policies that ultimately closed these coverage gaps, increased overall coverage, and lowered the family's total premiums by 20 percent. I also helped implement an annual policy review process for the family and their insurance agent, which would prevent these kinds of liability issues in the future.

Wealth management requires seeing the whole picture—not just your assets but also all the aspects of wealth that make your life truly valuable. This holistic approach has become more and more relevant in today's shifting financial landscape. In the last chapter, I talked about the complexities of wealth and the risks facing high-net-worth individuals and families. With all these potential threats to one's wealth, it's more important than ever to have some-one who not only understands the many disciplines pertaining to wealth management but who can also navigate them, build synchronized solutions, and coordinate with other professional advisors.

CHAPTER 3

Invest in the Future,
Not the Past

TRADITIONALLY, INVESTMENT ADVISORS have used models that look to the past to project the future. Though these methods have been industry standards for decades, they were developed over fifty years ago and can prove faulty during transitional times. I believe these models are flawed in a number of ways; unfortunately, they are still applied inappropriately and relied upon too heavily.

For the past several decades, financial advisors have been using a model called Modern Portfolio Theory. In the 1950s Harry Markowitz changed investment thinking by establishing a more analytic and quantitative approach to portfolio

construction. Diversification has long been recognized as an essential part of reducing risk. In
business, in life, and in portfolio management,
it's just common sense to not keep all your eggs in
one basket. Modern Portfolio Theory was the first
real attempt to quantify diversification by examin-
ing annual rates of returns, the volatility of asset
classes, and the correlation of returns between asset
classes. Using these three basic measurements, the
theory is designed to optimize an asset allocation
in order to achieve the highest returns at the lowest
level of risk. Modern Portfolio Theory relies heavily upon the benefits of diversification. The basic
idea is that when one asset group is doing poorly,
other assets are doing better—and vice versa. If
assets are not correlated to each other, they don't
move up and down at the same time; by definition,
they move up and down at different times. This
can reduce a portfolio's risk. On the other hand, if
all or most of your assets move in the same ways at
the same times, then when the market goes down,
most things in your portfolio lose value at the

same time and you have very little in your portfolio that's going up to cushion the fall. The investment advisory industry is, to a large extent, built on this theory. When a financial advisor provides a client with an asset allocation recommendation, they are almost always using Modern Portfolio Theory.

Some shortcomings of this theory have been identified. One problem is that the inputs used typically rely heavily on historical observations, meaning that the output—and the recommendations that flow from that output—will be quite dependent on the historical data used. Oftentimes, the models give more weight to more recent data— this can be a problem when a major crisis strikes, a long cycle ends, or the investment environment shifts. The model also assumes consistency (even certainty) about average rates of return and correlations between asset groups, as well as a number of statistical measurements, even though historical data can actually change over time. The fact is that correlations, rates of returns, and volatilities—the building blocks of this theory—are not consistent over time. Furthermore, a small difference in these assumptions can have a large impact on the model's results. So, if advisors rely primarily on Modern Portfolio Theory to generate recommendations, the results can be very flawed.

Anyone who was invested during the financial rollercoaster of the past several years can understand how this methodology comes up short during extreme events or shifts in market environments. Think back to the year 1999 and try to remember your expectations then—recall the reports you were shown, the asset allocation recommendations you received, and the estimated annual returns that were used in your financial plan. Did things work out the way those models predicted? Probably not. Remember, at the turn of the millennium, optimism was very high and the outlook seemed quite rosy. This sentiment was based on the market trends of the late '80s and '90s, a time when the economy was less volatile, growth was healthy and rates of returns were above average. However, a series of events (the dot-com bubble bust,

September 11th, a series of large-scale frauds and bankruptcies, the housing crash, and ultimately the financial crisis and "Great Recession" that began in 2007) dissipated the excessive optimism of the late 1990's to the extent that by 2009, extreme fear and pessimism was the norm. Over the past decade, the limitations of Modern Portfolio Theory have been exposed for all to see.

What happened in 2008: historical correlations between asset classes suddenly shifted and most asset classes started moving in the same direction. Unfortunately, the direction was down. After peaking in late 2007 (above 14,000), the Dow Jones Industrial Average began to fall, eventually plummeting below 6,500 in March of 2009 (stock markets had fallen well over 50 percent). While Modern Portfolio Theory and diversification did help during this time, overall it did not function in the way it should have on paper—diversification simply did not help enough. Many clients saw their portfolios drop lower than they ever would have expected. The traditional models, upon which financial advisors relied, broke down: most asset classes were going down at the same time, while correlations converged across the board.

Many advisors looked at the drawdown in their client's portfolios, and values had dropped more than they should have according to industry theory. At the depths of the collapse, emotions ran wild, clients began to panic and advisors often abandoned their investment strategies. The market had fallen well beyond many people's risk tolerance, and a lot of investors just wanted to sell everything and go to cash. This is not unusual at times of crisis— when things start falling apart, people start falling apart. Advisors, being human beings, are susceptible to these same emotions and mistakes, especially when a crisis shakes up the fundamentals of their investment strategies. It suddenly became apparent to many people that the rules may be changing or that trusted theories were inadequate. Even some of the smartest people in finance were left scratching their heads, and they spent several years trying to figure out what went wrong (I know; I heard and saw many a presentation from experts during the postmortem).

The economic crisis and the malaise of the past decade are painful reminders that the markets go through different cycles (cycles that sometimes last longer and go further than anyone thought possible). I can remember vividly being at a New Year's Eve party in 1999 as the ball dropped and we entered a new decade. Everyone was euphoric, economies were strong, the stock market was soaring, unemployment was at record lows, the U.S. was running a budget surplus, and the Internet was changing the world. It was then that it struck me: "Can things get any better? Is this what it was like in the Roaring '20s? Oh no! Could what followed then be around the corner now?" During the bear market of the early 2000s that soon followed, I wondered if we may be entering a long cycle of transition (historically characterized by low rates of return for stocks and increased volatility). In fact, I found evidence for this from a number of forward-thinking market historians (although at the time not many of us wanted to accept the notion of facing a decade or more of serious headwinds). If you had asked yourself in 2000, "Will the next decade look like the last decade?" we now know the correct answer was "probably not." Now, thirteen years later, will the next fifteen years be a repeat of the last fifteen years? Don't count on it! So why invest as if they will be? Advisors should not rely solely on purely quantitative tools but should also adjust for structural or long-lasting changes in markets. Sometimes markets are characterized with high or low growth rates. Sometimes markets are characterized by high-and-falling or low-and-rising interest rates. Likewise, markets can be characterized by inflation or disinflation/deflation. These different market regimes can lead to different outcomes than the standard models would have otherwise predicted.

Another issue with Modern Portfolio Theory has to do with how longer data sets are applied and relied upon. You've probably heard the term "stocks for the long run," right? Over the long run, stocks always outperform bonds, which in turn always outperform cash. Statistically, this has been true. But depending on when you start investing (particularly if stocks are expensive after many years of high returns), it could take decades until this notion bears out. That's typically what financial advisors mean by "the long run," but most investors cannot afford to wait twenty years or more until they make money.

The question you might ask is, "Why are so many advisors still counting on these tools if they know of these flaws?" Part of the reason is that change simply takes time because human beings resist change. Modern Portfolio Theory was developed fifty years ago, but it wasn't implemented consistently until about twenty years ago. It took thirty years for the investment community to recognize its usefulness and integrate it into the standard practices of the industry. However, once tools become industry standards, they are soon seen as conventional wisdom. In most fields, there is a degree of social validation that practitioners receive when they apply the "conventional wisdom" that most of their peers are using. John Maynard Keynes once wrote: "Worldly wisdom teaches that it is better for reputation to fail conventionally than to succeed unconventionally". The veneer of respectability for historically recognized methods can often overshadow their actual merits over time. Furthermore, professionals reduce career risk by sticking with industry standards. If you use recognized tools and models that everyone else in your field is using, then your career is at lower risk even if the results are poor. However, if you use a new model that is not yet broadly adopted, your career is at higher risk—even if your method succeeds over time (but not right away). It is scary to go against the grain, and so it is understandable that many advisors simply will not have the courage to do so. It's not that advisors are bad people or that they're consciously putting their careers ahead of their clients' interests (in fact, I believe this would be the rare case; in my experience, most advisors care dearly for their clients' welfare). It's just that financial advisors are human beings and are therefore susceptible to the same "groupthink" and herd-like behavior as professionals in any industry. This basic aspect of human nature is one reason why "conventional wisdom" and industry practices are slow to change.

For myself, I also find it uncomfortable to explore new things. However, I am fortunate to have the soul of an entrepreneur (highly motivated to improve products and services) and the mind of an engineer (insatiably curious to understand how things work) which have helped me adapt. As a young student, the following was a common interaction I would have with teachers and professors after class: "I know this does that—we just learned that today—but I want to know how it does it. What makes it work?" The teacher would reply and I would say, "Okay, now couldn't it work better this way instead?" This curiosity has lent me a natural capacity to think ahead, to look beyond the immediate present in order to figure out not just what has happened but also what could be next. At the end of the day, I—like most financial advisors out there—want my clients to be happier and more satisfied with their lives than they would be if I weren't working with them. To that end, rather than just fall back on "conventional wisdom," I look to stay competitive and keep my mind one step ahead—now that is what is really fun!

For more than a decade now, this philosophy has inspired me to use new tools and methodologies in the management of my clients' assets. Fortunately, a number of new strategies have been developed over the past several years that improve upon older models. Newer statistical tools and other sophisticated predictive methods are now available to address the shortcomings of older asset-allocation methodologies. Implementing these tools requires some extra work on the part of an advisor. It takes additional time and effort to perform the kind of analysis that is necessary to supplement traditional tools. Doing so involves taking a closer look at asset classes and considering them in the light of today's economic realities. Often, asset classes that have performed exceptionally well in recent histories are the ones that have become expensive (and investors should be skeptical of them). A forward-looking approach would cause you to trim those assets instead of buying them. Instead, focusing attention on relatively cheap asset classes that have underperformed for a time (and are unpopular and cheap as a result) would be a better idea. This is difficult to do for a lot of folks. The human mind is not well suited to making the kinds of tough choices that seem counterintuitive but are often the most financially beneficial.

Another step I take involves preparing for extreme events, which actually occur more frequently than statistical models would suggest. A good advisor must understand this reality and prepare for surprises and dramatic market events. Obviously, it's impossible to anticipate unforeseen events that are, well, "unforeseen." By definition, you do not see them coming; their timing is unpredictable. But it is possible for an advisor to know that these types of events are inevitable and to understand the need to build resilient portfolios that can survive them. This process requires "stress testing" portfolios for extreme events and observing what happens during those times. It's possible to garner information on the kinds of risks and returns that emerge during these downturns and to prepare clients for these potentialities by putting things in place that will mitigate the damage. Investors often fail to realize the interdependence (and common risk factors) that runs through seemingly different asset classes. During the short run, results can deviate substantially from long-run probabilities. Asset classes that are considered diversified can act very similar during extreme market events. Making it worse, I find that in history, strange things tend to happen in clusters. Successful wealth management is about survivability; you have to get through extreme events without severely impairing your finances.

As I mentioned earlier, it's also important to understand that markets have short-term and long-term cycles. Markets tend to oscillate between long periods of growth and long periods of consolidation (mostly going sideways with little real progress)—all of which are affected by larger cycles in the economy, investor psychology, rising/falling valuations, demographics and waves of innovation. I believe one of the most powerful factors affecting many of these cycles is investor behavior. When the market is doing well for a considerable amount of time, investor psychology grows more and more optimistic and stocks become more and more overpriced. Enthusiasm from past returns makes investors even more optimistic about future returns and prices of investments are bid up to a point where valuations no longer seem to matter. Eventually, optimism is so high that things truly "cannot get any better." Excessively high expectations eventually lead to marginal disappointment, which in turn leads to a realization that things "cannot stay this good"; "My investments are too expensive so I am going to sell." Prices begin to fall and more people start selling, leading prices to fall further, and so on, and so on. The virtuous up cycle of optimism thus morphs into a spiraling down cycle of pessimism, which will run its course until it too has become extreme. Eventually no one wants to invest and everyone feels like: "Things always go down, everyone loses money."

But the astute investor realizes: "Now investments are cheap!"

As an advisor, I must stay tuned to these trends as well as where we currently are along the spectrum of psychology (where we are in the cycle). When these trends go on for a long time, we are likely approaching a point when they will reverse themselves. At extremes of psychology and valuation, it is time to go against the herd. I'm not saying that it is possible for even the smartest investors to precisely time the peaks and troughs of these cycles (in fact, trends can continue on longer than one would ever expect). However, advisors can recognize when things are moving toward extreme levels. When discussing this, Benjamin Graham is attributed the following quote: "If you see that a man is very fat, it makes little difference that you are able to precisely calculate his exact weight to enhance your conclusion."

While history does rhyme, it does not exactly repeat itself nor does it move in a straight line. It is important to distinguish between these realities. Considering where we are in the cycles of history provides insight as to what to focus on next. Like the weather, it easy to sense the present (if it is raining, then carry an umbrella; you might not need it, but it is still a good idea) but much more challenging to predict the future. Meteorologists have gotten pretty good at predicting weather conditions a few days out. Beyond that ... not so good. As for financial forecasters on financial news stations ... they can report when markets are up or down, but they need a few more "financial weather satellites" before we can rely on their forecasts! We do know that there are seasons in every year. We know that summer is followed by fall, then winter, then spring. If we recognize what season we are in, then we can prepare for the one to follow (even if we don't have a calendar). When you see that it is fall (the leaves are turning and days are getting shorter), it's probably not a good idea to plant your seeds in the garden. After a long winter (the snow is starting to melt, and the days are getting longer), well ... it might be a good time to sharpen the garden tools and get ready to grow some crops.

Using newer tools and methods has helped navigate clients throughout the 2000s, making progress during a time when equity markets had one of their worst decades ever. When the financial crisis hit full force in 2008, it was these very tools that helped us to stay the course with clients. We did not predict or time the financial crisis. In fact, we were as surprised and shocked as anyone by how severe and widespread it became (nor did we expect governments to take drastic actions, some of which we believe made things worse). We did not prevent clients from losing value in their portfolios. We did not avoid making mistakes. However, we brought clients through the storm with much less damage than if we had not used these additional tools. As a result, we had a shallower hole to dig out of and it took less time to get portfolios back to their peak values (and beyond).

The bottom line—looking in the rearview mirror simply doesn't work much of the time (the view in the mirror is often different than the view through the windshield). More than ever, you need an investment strategy that acknowledges the shortcomings of conventional wisdom and existing methodology and utilizes newer tools to improve upon them. It's not that the standard models of the investment industry are wrong; it's just that they are incomplete and were never intended to provide permanent answers. Financial advisors need to take these extra steps to counteract the deficiencies of older investment models, take a forward looking approach based on market cycles and behavioral finance, actively manage risk and adapt to changing conditions. In chapter 8, I will describe in more detail some of the tools we use to build truly resilient portfolios.

CHAPTER 4

Don't Let Your Emotions Dictate Your Financial Future

WHEN I WAS first starting out in my career as a financial advisor, one of my mentors gave me a piece of advice. "Matt," he said, "I don't care who you work with or how smart they are, the truth is that most people don't know what to do with their money." My initial thought was that this was a rather low view of people. Most of the clients I'd worked with so far seemed to have a solid understanding of the markets and definite ideas about how they wanted to invest their money.

It wasn't until years later that I understood what my mentor was really talking about. It wasn't that people were ignorant, and it wasn't that they were incapable of analyzing investment opportunities. The challenge was that their emotions often got the better of them. They became too optimistic and enthusiastic after investments had gone up, and too fearful and skeptical of investments that had gone down. Their feelings about their investments were more affected by recent performance than by the underlying fundamentals for the future worth of those investments.

In my experience over the years, I've found that human emotions are probably the largest detriment to investor performance. I believe that the investment industry should and will be focusing more and more on the impact of psychology on managing wealth—and I predict that we'll see this becoming a much bigger component of wealth management in the future. Here is a concern that I have always had: most of the economic models taught to economists and applied today in the financial markets rely upon the assumption of rational (unemotional) human behavior. The Capital Asset Pricing Model, the Efficient Market Theory, Modern Portfolio

Theory, etc., all rely heavily on this assumption. However, I've never really believed that the assumption holds true, and new models have emerged that take this into account. The Capital Asset Pricing Model claims that if there is perfect information and all actors are rational, the price of a security will always reflect its intrinsic value. In other words, rational people who have all the relevant information at their fingertips would never pay more or less for a security than it's actually worth. Of course, in the real world, this isn't the case—people do not always act rationally. Psychologists and experimental economists have been verifying this for years and they have documented a number of ways in which actual human behavior deviates from rational behavior (these human biases include *overreaction*, *loss aversion*, *overconfidence*, as well as a number of mental shortcuts that lead to irrational decisions). I believe this is a primary reason why economics cannot be applied the same way as other sciences such as physics or mathematics. Economics involves systems of millions of human interactions, making things much more complex than systems involving inanimate objects—governed by known laws, formulas and relationships.

The deepest (and therefore least controllable) parts of the human brain developed first (mostly during a primal time when humans were not faced with the complexities of the modern world). This primitive part of our mind is designed to automatically seek things that we feel will improve survival and avoid the opposite. Chemicals and circuits in our brains reinforce this so that we unconsciously crave rewarding feelings and avoid what we perceive as risky or threatening. This reflexive system allows us to quickly identify patterns, react without thinking, focus on the most critical stimuli and identify the most immediate threats. This served us well in less complicated times as these instinctive responses conserved energy (it takes a lot of energy to consciously and reflectively think how to respond) and allowed us to react instantly. Unfortunately, when the old brain mixes with the modern world, it tends to leap to automatic, unconscious, uncontrollable and usually inaccurate (irrational) conclusions. Our impressive ability to recognize and react to simple patterns does not work well when applied to the more complex systems of modern times. These natural impulses may have served us well on the savannah, but they don't translate into effective skills when it comes to investments. Nobody likes to think of themselves as driven by their emotions (let alone the reptile-like part of their brain). However, it can be shown that this is exactly how most people respond to complex investment decisions. When the markets are down, most investors see "danger"—so they panic and run away. When markets are up, feelings of wellbeing (and even greed) instinctually kick in and people want to invest more. I believe that money is often made and wealth often preserved by going against our gut instincts. Warren Buffett once advised investors to "be fearful when others are greedy and greedy when others are fearful." In other words, making smart investment choices often requires us to think counterintuitively. Investors have to realize that their knee-jerk reactions often have little to do with the true merits of an investment opportunity. In fact, knowledge and studied analysis alone do not necessarily translate into investment success unless you are able to control emotion.

Let's look at mutual funds to demonstrate. For almost twenty years, the research organization DALBAR has conducted a quantitative analysis of investor behavior that measures the effects of investor decisions to buy, sell and switch into and out of mutual funds. Each year, DALBAR compares the performance of mutual funds to the actual results that investors, who invested in those same funds, received. Consistently, this research shows that the investors receive only a fraction of the actual returns of the funds they were invested in. Why is this? The studies indicate that it is primarily due to the emotionally driven behavior of investors. People become more optimistic and confident when a fund has been performing well. In response to these feelings, investors tend to buy (or buy more), chasing past results and ultimately "buying high." When a mutual fund goes through a down cycle, investors become pessimistic and fearful. In response to those feelings, investors tend to sell, in effect, locking in losses and "selling low." In other words, most investors are missing a big portion of the rate of return on their investments not because of the actual performance of the investment, but because of their emotional buying (high) and selling (low). It has been said that investing is the only market where customers sell when prices drop but buy more when prices rise.

I believe that mass psychology is the primary cause of market volatility. The fact that prices of assets fluctuate far more than their underlying value is the best evidence of this phenomenon. Earnings of companies do not fluctuate 20 percent from quarter to quarter, yet stock prices can easily do so. Economic growth (such as GDP) does not fluctuate 50 percent from one year to the next, yet market prices can easily do so. If it weren't for the vacillating optimism and pessimism of investors, the market should track earnings growth and the economy more closely than it does.

Creating a Buffer of Expertise

Obviously, it's impossible to completely separate your emotions from your finances. But you can create distance between your emotions and your money by putting experts in the middle. If you're managing your wealth on your own, then your money is directly exposed to your emotions with no offsetting influence—that's simply asking for trouble. But if you have advisors and experienced professionals who create a buffer of expertise, you're much more likely to avoid emotional reactions and big financial mistakes.

During the financial crisis, I had a number of clients who would have made painful mistakes if I hadn't helped them manage their emotions. A number of clients were saying, "I just want to get out." A lot of folks were panicking, and some people really thought the world was coming to an end. "Just sell everything, the whole banking system is going to collapse!" they said. "The market is going down to nothing!" It took real effort to calmly explain why this was unlikely to happen. I spent a lot of time during the crisis years reading, studying, and gathering concrete information about what was taking place and mapping out the facts for clients. This process allowed me to provide some rational thought and peace of mind to help clients manage their emotions.

One of the most important aspects of my job is to insulate my clients' reactionary impulses from their investment strategies and look at the facts for what they are. Occasionally, when a client is still so distraught that I cannot assuage their fears, I need to take those fears (i.e., "Just sell everything the whole banking system is going to collapse!") and walk the client through to their logical conclusion.

"Ok," I say. "Well, what are you going to do with the cash if you liquidate your portfolio?"

"I'll take it home, put it in a safe, and ride out the storm," they might respond.

"All right, and what are you going to do next?

If the banking system collapses, that means that within days, there won't be any food in the grocery story. That would mean your power will go off and the water will stop running."—"Well, I have hurricane supplies in the garage … you know, extra food and water."—"Yes, but if the system collapses, your neighbors are going to be knocking at your back door, trying to feed their starving kids. You may need to get a gun and a guard dog on the way home today. Do you really think that's where we're headed? Is that the world you want to plan for? If so, there are more important things to do than just selling your portfolio. Think *Mad Max*, which is what will happen if the system collapses. If it does not collapse, and I truly believe it will not, then it will recover from these panic levels." At this point, they would usually acknowledge that end-of-the-world scenario wasn't a probable outcome. I've found that sometimes it's best to simply acknowledge people's pain and carry their fears to their logical ends (look into the abyss), so that people can put things into perspective and work through their emotions.

Over the years, I have discovered that another way to help manage emotional reactions is to talk about fear and panic (and the circumstances that will trigger them) with clients ahead of time, so we can preemptively prepare how we will respond when an unforeseen event does occur. I tell each of my clients, "The worst time to sell investments is when everyone is panicking (which is precisely the time you are most likely to be really scared). So, at some point, and I don't know when, we're going to be sitting here and your portfolio is going to be down twenty, twenty-five percent, and you're going to want to sell something or even everything. At that point, I'm going to remind you of this conversation we're having right now, so you can mentally bring yourself back to this time and recall why you should not give in to your emotions." Having that conversation up front helps clients understand how their behavior and their emotions could negatively impact them. These talks make them aware of their own emotions and prepare them for the bad times in advance, so that they're better able to manage their reactions. I believe that investors' tolerance for risk actually changes over time. When things are going well, investors tend to feel that they can tolerate more risk than when their portfolio is actually going down.

I also try to steer my clients away from investments that—although they have a very high rate of return—will fluctuate too much for them to tolerate. Many times, I've had to say, "Listen, I know that *emerging markets* fund has gone up 20 percent a year and you'd like to put all your money in it, but you will not be able to handle it when the market drops and it goes down 70 percent. You just can't handle that." Honest and up-front conversations like these help protect my clients from making the kinds of decisions that will cause them too much pain and stress in the future.

Doing the Tough Thing

Of course, financial advisors are human beings too. We too experience emotions during market crashes and other startling events. To some extent, we feel the pressure during difficult times even more acutely than the investors themselves, since the collective fear and anxiety of all of our clients is projected upon us.

After all, advisors have people's lives—their retirement, their way of life, and the legacy intended for their children—resting on their shoulders. There are hundreds of people looking to each of us, counting on us, and that pressure can be overwhelming. In some ways, being a financial advisor is similar to being a doctor: during a bear market, it's like there's an outbreak of the plague; our clients are getting very sick but the medicine isn't working yet.

I believe this is one of the reasons why few people who set out to become a financial advisor succeed in making a career of it: Not many people can handle the emotional side of the investment business. It requires shouldering the emotions of a lot of people while managing your own emotions so you don't succumb to the same panic or excessive enthusiasm. It's crucial for financial advisors to maintain control of their own emotions, so that they can continue to make the rational decisions for the clients who are depending on them. Making tough decisions is what good financial advisors prepare themselves to do. It's incredibly easy for an advisor to take the path of least resistance. It's easy to let clients buy the latest hot stock (ignoring its expensive price) when investor excitement is high, but that's likely the wrong thing to do. The more difficult—and probably more beneficial—choice would be to make an investment that, while unpopular and out of favor, is attractively priced.

It's not easy to do the "tough" things (after all … they're tough!), but an important job of a financial advisor is to manage emotions and do what is best for clients. There are times—particularly during extreme events—when I've had to say to myself, "Look, today is going to be rough, but it's my job to be the rock—the voice of reason. I don't care how worried I am, how upset I am that things are scary out there. It's my job to NOT project these fears back to my clients. They have the luxury of venting to me; I do not have the luxury to vent to them.

It's my job to gather the strength to absorb their pain so they can get through these tough times." I think this is similar to how soldiers gird themselves for combat. I believe soldiers are just as scared as anyone would be. The difference is that they have mentally prepared themselves to keep it together and continue doing what needs to be done in the face of the carnage and danger. Their bravery is not a result of the absence of fear but comes from their ability to function in the presence of that fear (we could all take a lesson from them).

Knowledge Breeds Confidence

My personal experience is that knowledge breeds confidence. The more I can educate clients about how markets work, and the cycles that they go through, and what is going on now, the more confidence I believe those clients will have in their investment strategy. It seems to me that people tend to get more emotional about things they don't completely understand—I think that's basic human nature.

I feel that the time I invest preparing clients to be more confident is well spent. After all, if my clients are more knowledgeable, comfortable, and confident, then they will be less reactionary. Most of my clients reach a point of confidence where they rarely react to short-term, news-driven events. That ultimately pays off in extra time I have to devote to the analysis, research, and skills that allow me to provide them with better results, service and proactive recommendations. In my professional practice, we also keep our clients informed through regular communication. If the market has a big move in a day, we send out a notice by email to everyone, explaining what is happening. So, if a client comes home and turns on CNBC and finds that the market is up or down significantly, they already have our thoughts as to what is going on (right at their fingertips). Whether markets are turbulent or not, we write a weekly newsletter and quarterly "Global Market Commentary." These include our views regarding what has happened, what is happening, and what we think will be happening. All of this allows us to keep our clients informed and breeds confidence and peace of mind year-round.

In 2010, I hired a consulting firm to coach my team through a unique set of in-depth interviews with some of our best clients. Over the course of a year, we asked clients a few very candid and open-ended questions. One question we asked was, "Of all the services we provide to you, what do you value the most and why?" We meticulously documented their responses (word for word) and then took a thoughtful look at what each of them said. From this we found a number of consistent phrases and we were surprised by the results. We expected things like, "my financial plan," "my rate of return," "the results in my portfolio." However, almost every client's answer included, "confidence," "peace of mind," and "I can sleep at night." I don't believe that necessarily comes just from financial results. Rather, I believe that confidence and peace of mind are generated through the time we spend helping our clients understand their wealth through the knowledge, education, and communication we provide to them. Armed with this, our clients are able to make the best possible decisions for the future of their wealth.

I have come to understand that people work with a financial advisor primarily because they want to feel secure and confident in their financial decisions. Regardless of how rich you are, if you don't have peace of mind, you're not leading a joyful life. If your money is causing you worry, stress, and confusion, you may be happier buying a boat, gifting away your money, and moving to Costa Rica to live on the beach.

It goes without saying that in addition to peace of mind, our clients also want concrete results. Fortunately, these two things go hand in hand. As I mentioned, getting results depends largely on an investor's ability to remain calm and rational in turbulent times. If clients don't stay calm—if they don't stay the course, then they're not going to get the results that they should. You can pick all the right investments, but they won't do you any good if you bail out on them the first time they drop in price. If you handle your emotions poorly, you risk losing a lot of money—as well as missing out on potential returns.

The Power of Optimism

Today I believe the number one emotion that clouds the future is pessimism. Even though we're coming out of the "Great Recession" and things are starting to improve, a lot of people are still scarred by their experiences of the past decade, fearful that our world has permanently changed and we face insurmountable problems. There's a general sense that the best days are behind us and the future will remain forever dangerous and bleak. Such pessimism and fear can be just as detrimental to an investor's decision-making as excessive optimism. There's an old dictum about autoracing: "If you think about hitting the wall, you're going to hit the wall." The same logic holds true for investment opportunities: Cynicism ultimately becomes a self-fulfilling prophecy because you'll overlook the opportunities that do exist.

I believe today's pessimism is shortsighted. When you look at history, it becomes clear that recessions and tough times have functioned as cleansing periods—times during which inefficient and outdated modes of business are replaced with innovation and a renewal of the entrepreneurial spirit. This happened during the 1970s, when the industries that disappeared were then replaced (in the '80s and '90s) with game-changing technologies like personal computing, the Internet, and mobile telecommunications industries. No one could have imagined these new industries before they emerged (outside of a science fiction novel). I believe a similar process is taking place today with the emergence of "Big-Data" analytics, energy innovations, 3-D printing, genomics, and other technological developments. These emerging technologies promise to create new jobs and deliver a substantial boost to our GDP over the next decade. The reality is we're approaching a time where more optimism is warranted.

When clients express to me their worries about the future, I ask them to think about the big picture.

There are currently seven billion people on this planet, and every day these seven billion people wake up and go out into the world and try to make things better for themselves. This is ultimately what makes economies grow—it's what creates progress, technological innovation, and improved standards of living. And when you're invested, you own a share of that process. You're participating in that journey of global growth, renewal and hope, and you're getting returns based on that collective effort. When you think about this larger picture, it's difficult not to reclaim some level of optimism. Sure, sometimes there are setbacks and progress slows down, stalls, or even goes backwards for a while.

Most of the time, you can't control the circumstances around you, but you can always control your attitude. You ultimately get to choose how you think about the world around you, about the future, about how you are going to proceed. Your emotions can be your biggest detriment but managing your mindset can be your biggest asset. In today's economy, it's easy to get sucked into the mass psychology of doom and gloom. However, by surrounding yourself with experts who bring fact-driven information into the decision-making process, you can avoid falling prey to these alarmist and emotional reactions and achieve the peace of mind that allows you to truly enjoy your wealth and optimistically position yourself for the future.

CHAPTER 5

Manage Your Risks

INVESTING IN THE real world is about much more than just average returns; it is also about the risk along the way. Remember what I mentioned in chapter 4: If a portfolio is too volatile, you will likely never obtain the average return of that portfolio. Think of it like this: Turn up the oven to 200 degrees and set your freezer at zero, then put your head in the oven and your feet in the freezer. Your average body temperature may be normal, but the extremes at each end will kill you. Building a portfolio just based on long-term averages is like dressing every day based on the annual average temperature or climate of a region without considering the season or even the weather that day (if it's snowing outside, you should be adaptable enough to put on a coat and gloves).

In chapter 3, I discussed the limitations of traditional risk-management tools and the weaknesses that have been exposed within models such as Modern Portfolio Theory. Fortunately, thanks to advances in technology and expanded access to data, new tools have emerged to augment these outmoded methods of managing risk.

One of these tools is the "stress test," a method of measuring how an individual security—and therefore a portfolio of securities—will likely react during certain periods of market stress. By "stress," we mean extreme events: things like a sudden drop in the stock market, a currency disruption, episodes of war and terrorist attacks, interest rate shocks, inflation, deflation—basically, any kind of sudden and unexpected event in the marketplace that would impact securities and investments—often in a negative way. Within my practice, we now use institutional-quality risk analytics that provide portfolio-level statistics from the security level up, using the absolute risk of each position and its correlation with all other securities within the portfolio.

Stress testing has been around for some time, but in recent years the technology that performs these tests has become incredibly granular and robust. The early versions of these tools just tested overall markets or asset groups (such as U.S. stocks, international stocks, and bonds), but it wasn't until about three years ago that data became available at the security level to stress test actual and distinct portfolios. Before then, the data and software were not available to handle these kinds of computations. As an advisor, I'm always looking for the most accurate and state-of-the-art tools to measure risk—and that's where we're at right now with this new technology.

We test multiple stresses on a client's portfolio to see how the portfolio would have actually been affected. For example, let's say you have a portfolio that consists of mutual funds, stocks, bonds, and even hedge funds. We can actually measure how each one of these securities reacted during multiple types of stressful environments in the past. Measuring potential stresses at the individual security level provides us with a strong understanding of what the entire portfolio would do during such events. Because we can see which individual investments are driving the effects on the overall portfolio, we can use this information to fine-tune the portfolio as a whole, helping it perform better during extreme events.

As we manage clients' assets, we allow for a limited amount of risk, based on the client's risk tolerance. We'll regularly test the portfolio for ten to fifteen different types of extreme events—things like hyperinflation, the invasion of Iraq, the collapse of Long-Term Capital Management, September 11th, the Lehman Brothers collapse, the Asian currency crises, the tech bubble bust in 2000, and the Great Recession of 2008–2009. Then, we make sure the "drawdown"—the actual drop in value of the portfolio in real dollar terms—does not exceed a certain threshold. We perform these stress tests on a regular basis as a way of monitoring how much downside risk a portfolio is exposed to. If we are looking to add new positions or new allocations, we stress test at that time as well to see if we are introducing new or unacceptable risks to the portfolio.

Unfortunately, a very small number of advisors are using these kinds of tools today. Since the software can be very expensive, one of the biggest barriers is cost. Using these tools also requires some training, in order to ensure that the advisor uses them correctly. As with any software or computation, if you input the wrong questions, you get the wrong answers. In addition to cost and the time required for training, advisors are hesitant to change their standard way of doing things. Advisors, like professionals in any field, tend to be slow to adopt new tools. In general, it's human nature to resist change and the possibility of doing things differently.

We've been using the newest stress test tools for almost three years, and we've found them to be an invaluable resource. In a review meeting, we can run this software and show clients the actual drawdown of their portfolio under certain scenarios.

Seeing the results of a stress test allows a client to consider the kinds of events they are most worried about, and understand the impact such events would have on their portfolios, based on how the securities were affected by similar events in the past. Sometimes clients look at the results and say, "You know, I thought I could handle that. But if that's what would really happen, then I need a more conservative portfolio." Or vice versa—some clients consider the results and say, "Oh, that's nothing. A drawdown of fifteen percent? I've been through that before. In fact, I've been through worse before, so I'd like to make my portfolio a bit more aggressive."

The great thing about these tools is that they are based on actual, real-world data of how securities have reacted to a wide range of stressful events. By contrast, Modern Portfolio Theory—the traditional tool used for managing risk—is more theoretical in nature and measures volatility only at the asset class or index level. To quantify risk, Modern Portfolio Theory relies on a measure known as "standard deviation," which is basically how much the actual rate of return of a certain asset class deviates from its average at any given point in time. This includes deviations above (or better than) average, when in real life, investors are mostly concerned with deviations to the down side.

If you can take yourself back to college statistics class, you probably recall learning about the "bell curve." There are many cases where data tends to cluster around a central value (or average value) with no bias left or right. In other words, there's a "normal distribution"—that's the shape of the normal bell curve (think of a side profile of a bell). As you move to the left or right of that center of the bell curve, the sides drop, so there is a smaller area (fewer occurrences) under the bell shape as you move away from middle (the middle represents the average). In this way, statistics can measure variation because there are laws that correspond to normal distributions. For instance, 68 percent of all occurrences will fall within one standard deviation of the average, while 95 percent will fall within two standard deviations and 99 percent will fall within three standard deviations. Traditional tools like Modern Portfolio Theory use statistics to theoretically ascertain the likelihood of X amount of loss to a portfolio in an extreme event. The problem with this method is that markets don't have normal distributions. When it comes to market return distributions, the bell curve is actually shorter and a lot wider than "normal"—they call these wider ends "fat tails." This means that in the real world, extreme occurrences happen far more often and are much more damaging than theory (based on statistical models) would suggest.

During the late-2000s financial crisis, many financial firms suffered far greater losses than their statistical models predicted. They were exposed to more risk than they thought possible. I believe this happened, at least in part, because many of the tools they were using were theoretical in nature. Financial firms take great pains to control their exposure to losses as they balance assets and liabilities. To do so, they hire a lot of very smart mathematicians from Ivy League schools to apply statistical calculations and model the probabilities and degree of loss during worst-case scenarios—that's how these firms were estimating how much risk they were exposed to every day: on their balance sheets. However, the statistics underestimated how probable or how damaging a national collapse in housing prices would be in real life. That's why a lot of firms came under stress during the financial crisis.

We know that markets are not "normal," so statistics and math that assume "normal distributions" are not always an accurate way to predict outcomes. Also, in my experience, I've found that these more abstract calculations do not seem real to most clients. If I explain to a client that bonds have a standard deviation of six, they typically ask, "What does that actually mean?" I find that most clients are very practical—they essentially want to know how much their portfolio could go down if an unexpected event actually happened. While stress tests cannot predict the future, they are very accurate at measuring how bad things could get when things go bad. I believe that's as close as you can get to measuring how much risk exists in a portfolio at a given time.

These kinds of tests have been particularly useful recently, as we prepare for a rise in interest rates over the next several years. We've had thirty years of falling interest rates, and some are now almost at zero. So we know that the next thirty years are probably not going to look like the last thirty years—in fact, we're probably going to be dealing with the opposite. Because of this, we've been particularly concerned about how this environment of rising interest rates is going to affect our clients' portfolios. A basic rule of thumb is that a rise in interest rates causes a drop in bond prices. However, when you're managing portfolios of many different assets, it's more difficult to predict the effect on the portfolio as a whole—what happens to the bonds is one thing, but what happens to the portfolio as a whole, is another matter. As we run stress tests for rising interest rates on portfolios, some of the results have been quite interesting. We expected that U.S. government Treasuries would be purely affected by interest rates and that these assets would go down if interest rates rose. But it's been interesting to see how other securities react under those same conditions. By running the stress tests, we are seeing how rising interest rates actually affect many other income-producing investments positively over time—though it shocks them in the short run.

This knowledge has allowed us to position portfolios for rising interest rates without necessarily eliminating all income-producing securities from the portfolios. As a result, we've been able to keep income-producing securities in many of our portfolios, which is important for our clients' cash flow—all while minimizing the negative effects of rising interest rates. This is something that would have been impossible to measure had we been simply relying on the perceived rule of thumb (when interest rates rise, bonds goes down). It's a result I don't think we would have completely picked up on prior to using those tools, and it's helped us position portfolios for the future without eliminating fixed-income securities altogether.

These new methods of measuring and managing risk are a significant improvement because they are based on real life events and test individual securities. We can now model and stress test portfolios for virtually any negative event that one can imagine—whatever disaster a client is most fearful of. Ultimately, this kind of risk management is more meaningful to clients than theoretical models and statistics. Stress tests enhance investor confidence and allow us to prepare our clients for extreme events and minimize potential threats to their wealth.

CHAPTER 6

Build a Collaborative Team

ONE OF THE most important elements of effective wealth management is coordination of advice. As I pointed out earlier, in today's economic landscape, there are a number of factors that complicate the process of managing wealth, which means it's more important than ever for the various experts who work for wealthy families to synchronize their efforts.

Typically, wealthy families have multiples advisors who specialize in different areas or disciplines—attorneys, tax specialists, insurance agents, and the like. A family could find the best specialist in each field, but if these experts do not work in harmony, the results can be dreadful. Imagine an orchestra comprised of the best musicians in the world—each player might be a virtuoso, but if they're not playing from the same sheet of music, it sounds awful. Think about how a symphony sounds when the musicians are warming up; playing on their own without the direction of the conductor—it is painful to listen to. Likewise, if you're cooking a gourmet meal, it's critical to know what things go together, in what proportions, and in what order. You could have the world's best and most expensive ingredients, but unless you combine the right ones in the right way, it's not going to taste good. The same principle holds true when it comes to accounting, law, estate planning, insurance, and the other disciplines involved with wealth management: if these different areas are not coordinated, they're not going to achieve good results—one component may end up counteracting another.

A lot of people do not appreciate the importance of successful collaboration. For example, I'll ask a new client about their estate planning, and the client will typically assure me that they've done extensive planning in this area—and indeed they often have.

But when I take a closer look, it frequently turns out that the elaborate plan was never implemented properly with respect to asset accounts, the family business, or insurance policies. In other words, the estate planning would not end up working the way the family expected it to, because the plan hadn't been coordinated among all of their advisors and specialists. Often, a client's previous financial advisor simply failed to initiate cross communication with the family's other specialists. Mistakes are easy to make, but I've found that a lot of advisors and specialists actually favor working in isolation for a number of reasons.

Egos are one issue. Keep in mind, the best lawyers, tax advisors, and financial advisors—top performers who've spent years honing their skills in highly competitive environments—tend to be strong-minded personalities. If another advisor starts reviewing their work, there's the fear of criticism which, if brought to the client's attention, might make the advisor look bad. Nobody's perfect, after all, and everyone can make mistakes. Also, regardless of the talent and expertise of any individual professional, there are often things that can be improved upon when someone else takes a second look. So it is natural for an advisor to feel uneasy if their work is being "scrutinized" by another professional. It's important to work with advisors who are sensitive to this. If not, the advisor could easily offend your other advisors and make them defensive. Personally, if I see something in another discipline that appears that it could be improved, I try to communicate my thoughts in such a way that the other advisor doesn't feel threatened (after all, I might not understand things in the right way to begin with). My priority is always to make sure I understand the other advisors' objectives and support them in providing great service to the client. Trust building amongst the advisory team is crucial—it takes constant communication, a spirit of good faith cooperation, and an unwavering respect for others.

I try to demonstrate this good faith through my actions. When I see something that appears that it could be improved upon, I always strive to maintain (and even enhance) that other advisor's relationship with the client. A first step is to verify that I fully understand and appreciate their advice and strategies for that client. I just ask, "I see that you have set this up in this way, can you help me understand how this works and the objective for this strategy?" At worst, I reach a better understanding of how things fit into the client's total wealth management. At best, the other advisor says something like, "You know, Matt, now that I am going through this with you, I see that we could tweak some things to make it even better. After all, a few things seem to have changed with the client's situation since I spoke to them last." This kind of conversation is a win-win not just for the client, but for the advisors as well. I also respect the professional's time by informing myself—to the best of my ability—about a topic before I approach the subject with the other advisor. There is nothing more frustrating for an attorney or accountant than to have to re-explain a concept to a financial advisor who is uniformed about the very subject he/she is questioning. I believe financial advisors should focus on this type of cooperation in order to achieve the best outcomes for clients.

Another barrier to collaboration is inadequate cross-discipline competency. As I mentioned above, sometimes a financial advisor is not sufficiently fluent in other disciplines to really understand the other professional's field of work. Obviously, a financial advisor is not in a position to actually do the work of another discipline—that isn't their job. But they can understand enough about these other fields to be able to keep up with conversations, ask the right questions, and participate in the process of wealth management from other points of view.

For many financial advisors, those cross-discipline conversations can be a real challenge and quite intimidating. In my experience, advisors often fail to initiate important conversations with their clients because they are afraid of moving into a topic with which they're not entirely comfortable. For instance, an advisor might avoid engaging with their clients about succession planning. After all, there's a possibility that the client might say, "Hey, great question. Let me schedule an appointment with my lawyer, my CEO, my CFO, my tax guy, and my insurance guy. What does your schedule look like this Wednesday?" The reality is that it wouldn't feel comfortable being thrown into a room with these sophisticated, high-powered advisors, talking about complicated and technical techniques used in these other disciplines. It is understandable that advisors fear they might end up in a conversation outside their area of expertise, forced to weigh in on a subject they don't understand and are not completely comfortable discussing. Like most professionals, financial advisors want to look smart and competent to their clients. If an advisor is insecure in this way, they may avoid initiating or participating in these important discussions and simply hope for the best.

Building Trust

Personally, I believe that financial advisors could do a better job for clients if they invested the time to learn about these other fields and become comfortable with cross-discipline conversations.

It's true that this investment of time doesn't have an immediate payoff. After all, such a big sunk cost of time may not result in any direct compensation to the advisor until years down the road (or maybe not at all). It takes a longsighted approach and financial advisors can be relatively shortsighted (since they are subject to the near-term pressures of running their practice, attending to more immediate concerns and generating revenue). If an advisor carves out extra hours in the day or week, they will probably spend that time on direct sales or marketing.

Early in my career, I learned that if I wanted to build long-lasting relationships with my clients, I would have to address those areas of life they cared about the most. Through talking to my clients about what they truly value, I discovered that often, what's most important to them exists beyond my immediate specialty (management of their liquid investments)—it is their families, the business they built from the ground up, their legacy. I knew that if I wanted to positively impact those other areas of a client's life, I would have to learn more about the other disciplines that influenced them.

I have found that clients are better able to achieve true peace of mind when they know that the various areas affecting their wealth are being coordinated in a comprehensive fashion. On my end, this requires extra time and effort in the short run, but pays off in the form of deeper and more rewarding client relationships. My process leads to longer-lasting relationships—most of which extend across generations. By creating a broader knowledge base and demonstrating my ability to work with other advisors on these complex issues—whether it's transitioning through the sale of a business, or working with their kids on an estate plan—I've been able to provide my clients with a level of continuity through the generations. Consequently, these clients are more likely to leave their assets in my care. This is a testament to the importance of building lasting relationships. When a family puts you in place as a key advisor to their legacy, there's no greater compliment than that—in my book, that's the most serious and flattering gesture of confidence an advisor could receive.

Dealing with Tough Situations

Through this process of collaboration, I occasionally stumble on a problem that I need to address with another specialist or advisor in order to protect my client from potential harm. In the past, I've experienced a few situations where I discovered that one of the other professionals on the team had clearly made some mistakes or had not completed urgent work. These are tough situations to deal with. Obviously, I never want to jump to conclusions or make assumptions when the issue could simply be the result of a misunderstanding. Certainly, accusations never solve anything. I've learned in life that if you are going to accuse someone of something, be prepared for the relationship to end or become seriously damaged. Therefore, if I sense that something is amiss, I first approach the other advisor and tactfully ask them to help me connect the dots. "There's something here I didn't understand,"

I might say. "Can you help me understand this? I think I might be missing something. I've had some experience with this, but you are the expert." Or, "I was thinking this had been completed but maybe I am getting ahead of things." I like to give the other advisor every opportunity to identify a problem and improve things on their own. After all, the goal is to get the best results for the client, not to criticize the other advisor.

At this point, the other advisor might say, "You know what? Now that I am walking you through this, I'm thinking this could be done in a different way," or, "Now that you mention that, I was not aware of these new facts. In that case, I'm thinking we should make some adjustments." Most of the time these situations are resolved productively. So long as I make it clear that I'm not trying to do the other professional's job for them, that my goal is to achieve the best outcomes for our mutual client and ensure that the other advisor is seen in the best light, these exchanges are usually friendly and beneficial to everyone. Likewise, I often receive great feedback from other advisers when we collaborate. Many times, while reviewing a client's financial/estate plan with the client's other advisors, they will point out things that I missed and suggest improvements that would benefit the client. It never hurts and often helps to review things with a client's other advisors to get their feedback.

There are times, however, after such conversations when it becomes clear that another advisor is not doing the job correctly. In some cases, I've discovered that an advisor is actually trying to mislead the client. I'm always hesitant to accuse people. However, if it's clear that another professional is doing something questionable or even detrimental to the client, I consider it my duty to have a frank conversation with that person. "Look, we have to get this back on track."

Once, I discovered that an accountant who worked with one of my clients hadn't filed the family's tax returns. I approached them about this, and they said they would take care of it. But then, several months later, I found out that the returns still hadn't been filed. I called the accountant and said, "Look, those tax returns weren't filed for some reason and you said they were. We have to get this fixed." Fortunately, we were able to resolve this issue without troubling the client. However, in some cases, I've had no choice but to inform the client. In my opinion, this should be the last resort—I try to give other advisors every chance to remedy issues first. But I do have a certain obligation to the client and if I've exhausted all other options, I cannot, in good faith, withhold information about something that would be harmful to them.

The worst scenario is when I find that malfeasance or even a crime has occurred. If that's the case, I'm ethically (and often legally) bound to inform the client. Certainly, things are not always black or white. However, I try to keep in mind a couple of principles. Number one: I'm always working to get the best outcome for my client and to keep their best interest in mind. Number two: I try to honor the field of specialty of other advisor and give them every opportunity to do good work on their own initiative. I never step in between a client and their other advisors unless I absolutely have to in order to save the client from getting hurt. In my experience, true malfeasance is rare (although more common than clients would like to think). Remember, if you have wealth, then you are a likely target for criminals and swindlers. In light of this fact, you should conduct due diligence when hiring new advisors.

Accountability is just one of the many benefits that result from this type of cross-discipline coordination and communication. The more closely advisors work together, the more opportunities there are to fix problems, improve solutions, and achieve superior outcomes for clients. Fortunately, the majority of my work with other advisors has been rewarding and mutually beneficial. It takes a lot of effort to work as an effective team member—it requires educating oneself in other disciplines and putting egos aside. Nevertheless, the ultimate goal is to achieve the best outcome for the client. So long as everyone keeps that basic principle in mind, working together as a team can benefit everyone involved.

CHAPTER 7

Make Economics Your Friend

THERE'S AN OLD joke about economists: A student and his economics professor are walking across the campus, when they come across a ten-dollar bill lying on the ground. The professor keeps walking, and the student stops and asks his professor, "Hey, why didn't you pick up that ten bucks?" The economist looks back at the ten-dollar bill and says, "Well, if it were really there, someone would have already picked it up."

I think this joke speaks to a certain public perception of economists. Many people today tend to think of economists as detached experts who are so caught up in their models and theories that they've

THE FUTURE OF YOUR WEALTH

lost touch with the real world. To some extent, I can see why these stereotypes exist. Some economists are so isolated in their ivory towers that they no longer apply economics in ways that are relevant to the real world—in fact, many economic models make unrealistic assumptions just to make the real world conform to those models (instead of the other way around). So it's not surprising that economists are often thought of as people who are too smart for their own good and not smart enough for anyone else's.

The irony is that I was attracted to economics for precisely the opposite reason: I saw the field as a way to understand the more practical aspects of life. I've always been interested in business, capitalism, and entrepreneurship, and the study of economics was attractive to me because it was a way to comprehend how the world functions beyond simply reading abstract theories. Economics involved more science than fields like political science or philosophy, and I was always pretty good at math and science—applying the technical aspects of economics came easy to me. I have always had a firm belief that our world is a system rooted in people's motivations regarding how they live their lives, and that those motivations have a lot to do with making money, earning a living, securing shelter, food, and property—basically improving one's lot in life. That's essentially what makes the world go around, and economics seeks to explain how this process works. It seemed like an intriguing way to understand the world.

So I studied hard and earned two degrees in economics. I worked during the day and went to school at night, completing my undergraduate and then my graduate degree. This involved learning all the different economic theories formulated throughout history, from Adam Smith through the more modern models and schools of thought. It also involved evaluating the impacts of various historical events and economic policies. What's unique about economics is that it's both abstract and based in the reality of human behavior. Economics isn't a hard science like physics or mathematics, in which theories and postulates can be proven on paper with formulaic precision—after all, these scientific fields deal with inanimate objects. In physics, if you know the correct formulas you can pretty much calculate outcomes in the physical world. For example, if you know the laws of motion and their formulas, you can calculate the trajectory of a bullet—how far it will fly and where it will fall. I'll admit that mathematics and econometric formulas have introduced some objectivity to economic theory, but the precision and exactness that economist project upon their models today is way beyond reality. As I described in chapter 4, since human behavior is influenced by emotion (which is often not rational), and is dependent upon the behavior of others, economic models can only take you so far in predicting outcomes. While economics is based on mathematical formulas, models and statistics, it also takes into account real-world human behavior, which is not formulaic but rooted in empirical observation. In the real-world marketplace, you cannot simply say, "Well, if I have X, Y, and Z, I'm going to get

W." Markets don't work that way because people don't always behave logically or rationally. In fact, in order to work out on paper, many economic models must make "unreal" assumptions—otherwise the models become unstable. Sure, it helps to understand and interpret what factors might lead to certain outcomes. But at the end of the day, it's how humans *react* to things that ultimately determines outcomes. Once the limitations of economic theories are acknowledged in this way, economics can provide an invaluable background for anyone working within the financial markets.

You might ask, "Why aren't more economists financial advisors?" Well, think about the stereotypical economist: the nerdy intellectual, the number cruncher, the professorial type—someone who didn't have enough personality to become an accountant. The personality it takes to really excel in the field of economics is not necessarily the same personality that excels in a client-facing business like wealth management. Many people in the financial advisory industry have a background in sales, or even a business degree. Because financial advisors deal with people—their clients—as well as finance, they need two skill sets: One, they need to be very technically proficient with respect to finance and investing. Two, they have to be able to relate to people and deal with human emotions and psychology—that's mostly a sales skill. What I've seen in the financial advisory industry is that there are some people who are very technically proficient but have difficulty relating to individual clients. Then you have a whole lot of people in our industry who are excellent sales people—folks who have strong leadership skills and are really great at convincing clients to do certain things—but may not have a strong technical skill set.

I've never really thought of myself as a great sales person in the traditional sense. I'm not very pushy, I am brutally honest with clients, and I rarely assume that my unique vision of the world is the only way to go—I just don't have that personality. However, what I am able to do very well is relate to people on a personal level, empathize with their feelings, and communicate the technical aspects of wealth management and investing in a way that is understandable and makes sense to them. What's worked for me as an advisor is my ability to explain to clients what is a very complicated financial world in a simple and common-sense manner.

As I said before, I believe that knowledge breeds confidence. I consider myself fortunate that my background gives me a unique understanding of the markets and the cycles they go through. When I can impart that knowledge to my clients in a way that they truly comprehend, they are then much more confident in their portfolios and wealth management strategies. This in turn leads them to become more self-assured investors, allowing them to enjoy the peace of mind that comes from that confidence. Being able to educate clients about the management of wealth—explaining the logical relationships and logical structures that drive our investment strategies—has been invaluable.

The truth is that economists look at the world differently than most folks. When I pick up a copy

THE FUTURE OF YOUR WEALTH

of *The Wall Street Journal,* I'm probably less susceptible to the news of the day and more grounded
in the fundamentals of what's going on, or what's
causing the news. Let's face it: most of the news we
receive is packaged to be sensational and to "attract
eyeballs." If you take the news at face value, I don't
believe you will necessarily get a good sense of what
you should be doing with your money. Sure, the
pundits and columnists will try to explain why the
markets went up in a given day, but often they're
just picking reasons in order to provide an expla-
nation—their reasons are not necessarily the true
cause.

In fact, a lot of people today talk about the
financial market as though it's a mystical beast constantly working to confound us. When you hear the
day's stock market report, it's almost as though the
news people are personifying it—as if the market
has its own set of emotions (whether it's "anxious,"
"grumpy," "excited," or "tired") and exists independently from the people who are involved with it.
Experts and pundits can poke at the beast and try

to guess what it's going to do next, but the implication is that the market has a mind of its own and is smarter than any single investor.

On one hand, I understand the instinct to personify the market. After all, it really is the summation of all opinions out there, the total vote of every investor on the planet. But I'm hesitant to endow the market with too much autonomy because I believe it is ultimately psychology that drives market trends. The reality is that people tend to herd together—our moods and emotions are contagious. We seek social validation by observing others and acting like them and I believe that crowd behavior is the root cause of market swings. Euphoria breeds more euphoria, causing prices to rise too far. Pessimism breeds more pessimism, causing prices to fall too low. Sure, the market might be smart over time because it is the total opinion of millions of people. But these people are still human beings, and mass psychology can be very emotional and illogical in the short term.

Because of my economics background, I tend to

look at these mass psychology trends as an indica-
tion of where we are in a current cycle. In fact, I'd
argue that the tone of the financial headlines often
represents the opposite of what a smart investor
should be doing with their money. News networks
know that people tend to look for validation of
their feelings, so news stories often reflect the current mood of viewers. In this sense, the headlines
often mirror the mass psychology of the moment. If
extreme emotions can cause investments to become
too expensive or too cheap, I believe you should stay
tuned to investor psychology and think about how
to go against the crowd. If you are following the
theme of the headlines to manage your wealth, it's
probably not going to lead to good results.

Economics also provides tools and methods to
measure intrinsic value—an evaluation of what a
security should actually be worth, independent of
the market price that mass psychology has attributed to it. Comparing an unemotional assessment of
intrinsic value to the sometimes emotionallydriven
market price helps us gauge whether an investment

or asset class is expensive and should be avoided. The opposite is also true: If the market is dropping based on fear and pessimism—not a real change in the fundamentals—you may not want to follow the crowd and say, "Oh, the market's dropping! Let's sell." Instead, I tend to look at this and say, "The market's dropping, but it's really overreacting to underlying fundamentals, so maybe we should be buyers and go against the herd."

I often find that my background—my knowledge of history and various economic models and theories—provides me with a unique insight into market cycles, demographics, trends, and stages of development. If I can understand where we are right now, within a larger trend, I can usually get a better idea of what might emerge next—after all, identifying where we are in the current cycle is the key to predicting what's on the horizon. Think of the weather—it is hard to predict very far into the future. However, if you know what season you are in, you can figure out what season is coming next (even if you don't have a calendar). If it's springtime and the days are getting longer and the snow is melting, you have a pretty good idea that summer is coming and you might want to start planting your crops. Economics provides that kind of perspective.

I've found that it's greatly helpful to my clients when I can frame things for them in this way, explaining what I think is happening in the markets and why certain things are likely to happen in the future. If I can impart to my clients some of the essentials about how economics will impact their investments, then they have a better chance of understanding the potential future outcomes of their decisions. It's never perfect—obviously, nobody can predict the future—but this knowledge allows them to have the best shot at predicting the most probable future. Ultimately, that's the key to investing. Whether it's determining that an investment is too expensive (or cheap), or anticipating where new areas of growth will emerge, or discerning under what circumstances certain parts of the economy will thrive, the key to smart investments is informed foresight—and that's precisely what an economics background can offer.

If you can interpret and understand what's taking place in a particular market environment, you have a much better chance of navigating the future of your wealth.

CHAPTER 8

The Future of Your Wealth: Building the Resilient Portfolio

Moving Beyond the Numbers

TOO OFTEN, FINANCIAL advisors never move past formulaic financial planning, asking clients basic questions about income and cash flow. They ask questions like "At what age will you retire?" "What will your lifestyle cost?" "What major purchases to you expect?" "What are your investment assets?" "How much are you saving?" Don't get me wrong, these questions are very important. However, advisors often fail to ask the kinds of qualitative questions that get to the core of what that money means to the client and the aspirations they have for their wealth. Success means different things to different people, so when I sit down for the first time with a new client, I begin with with open-ended questions. The goal of these initial talks is to find out what's most important to the client and their family, whether it's the activities they engage in or the values that mean the most to them. I ask them "qualitative" questions—queries that move beyond the numbers and get to the heart of what wealth means to them. I ask things like, "What does it mean to you to be wealthy?" "What's the most important financial issue in your life right now?" "What's working well for you?" "What's not working so well and could be improved upon?"

One question I love to ask is, "In a perfect world, what would you like your money to do for you?" It's amazing—when I ask these open-ended questions, I can see people really pause and think. It's as if they had never before considered things in this way. The truth is that many wealthy people have been so busy running their business and their affairs that they rarely stop to think about what it's all for. What's the end game? Where is the journey taking them?

When will they know they have arrived? I hear all sorts of answers to this question: People say, "I really wish I didn't have to worry about my two young kids—I'd hate to think about what they would do if I wasn't around to help them out." Others say, "I really don't know what's going to happen to my business and employees after I retire," or, "I'm worried about the health of my parents." People begin to genuinely consider what they value in life when they think beyond the numbers.

These conversations are absolutely critical. For financial advisors, it's easy to get caught up in the numbers—to convince ourselves that everything revolves around rates of return and the values of assets. But the truth is that wealth means so much more because it ultimately provides (or fails to provide) for the things that matter the most in life. Many of these are intangibles—relationships, family, security, happiness, accomplishment, reputation, acceptance, success, philanthropy, peace of mind.

The answers to these questions provide context for the next step of our process, which is an in-depth analysis of what the family owns, as well as how they own it. We look at their current estate documents and their insurance coverage. This helps construct an accurate picture for the family of how they look financially. From there, we can identify steps that could be taken to move them towards their aspirations in more effective ways. We are able to suggest and discuss a number of strategies or solutions that will help them achieve their goals. We then bring in whatever resources and experts are needed—internal or external—to execute those solutions, and take the family to an even better place.

The Resilient Portfolio

What constitutes a resilient portfolio? In my view, this is a financial portfolio that can withstand unforeseen events. Obviously, it's not possible to predict extreme events, but we do know that they happen—if nothing else, the financial events of the past decade have been a painful reminder of this reality. As I pointed out in chapter 3, it's insufficient to merely use risk, return, and correlation forecasts to create robust portfolios. Seemingly diverse asset classes can have unexpectedly high correlations—a result of the significant overlap in their underlying common risk exposures.

Operating from this assumption, how can you build a portfolio that remains resilient when things go bad? Earlier, I discussed some shortcomings of Modern Portfolio Theory and other standard tools of the investment industry and suggested some extra steps that can be taken to supplement these old models. This includes stress testing actual portfolios for extreme events that have occurred in the past.

It's certainly important to build a robust portfolio through diversification. In fact, diversification has historically been the primary means to building resilient portfolios—and it is still important. However, we have seen that at times, it's just not enough to be spread investments across different asset classes. We need portfolios with sufficient investments that will respond positively in a variety of extreme events and market environments. Fortunately, there are quite a few tools at our disposal, and a good financial advisor can use these to prepare for the unexpected events that can occur from time to time.

Managing Liquidity: It's absolutely critical these days to have ample liquidity. You may have a diversified portfolio that, during an extreme event, doesn't go down as much as other assets. But if you're not liquid during those times, you may be forced to sell assets for much less than they are worth. Maintaining enough liquidity at all times is one of the keys to getting through tough financial times. We help clients analyze how much liquidity they would need during tough times and help them manage this as a separate pool of funds. Maintaining extra liquidity also allows you to capitalize on the exceptional values that emerge when markets are in distress and sellers are forced to liquidate holdings at low prices.

Holistic Asset Allocation: It is important to adjust your liquid investments to complement your total wealth. Here's an example: Imagine you have half your net worth in venture undertakings—your business, new startups, real estate projects. These are all higher-risk and illiquid assets. To maintain a robust portfolio, you have to acknowledge that your "risk" capital is largely concentrated in those enterprises. This means that you should maintain a lower than normal amount of risk in your liquid investment portfolio. If you're taking risk for growth in private enterprise, then your liquid investment assets should be more conservative than otherwise, in order to make your total net worth more robust and balanced.

Price Matters: Using a dynamic approach to asset allocation (instead of buy and hold), your portfolio should adjust according to cycles in the market. When prices are high or overvalued in one area, it's time to sell or trim these allocations; when prices are low or undervalued, it's a good time to buy or overweight that asset group. In my practice, we rely on a number of inputs from multiple sources to monitor under- and overvaluation conditions. We then adjust portfolios, applying tactical over- and underweights.

I mentioned earlier the limitations of conventional risk measurement tools and why it's important to stress test portfolios for a variety of extreme events. With sophisticated, institutional quality tools, we conduct regular stress tests of portfolios not only at the asset class level but also at the individual security/ product level. We are able to evaluate the absolute risk of each position and its correlation with all other securities within the portfolio. Downside risk measures allow us to evaluate the potential losses a portfolio might experience in a number of adverse events. These tests allow us to measure risk in both normal and stressed market conditions and measure the benefits of portfolio diversification as well as the effect of making selected changes to a portfolio from a risk perspective. Likewise, we separate downside risk from upside risk in our methodology. Modern Portfolio Theory treats upside and downside volatility as comparable risks. However, in the real world, upside risk is a good thing; it is downside risk that impairs wealth.

A Building Block Approach to Asset Allocation: I discussed earlier how seemingly diverse asset classes can have unexpectedly high correlations—a result of the significant overlap in their underlying common risk factor exposures. For instance, stocks and bonds could both be impacted adversely by rapidly rising inflation and interest rates, even though they are typically thought to have diversified risks. Rather than building portfolios by simply spreading assets across major asset classes, we build portfolios to diversify across risk factors, based on how the underlying assets are affected by those factors. We have found that the major factors that impact investments are inflation and deflation, growth and recession, as well as rising and falling interest rates.

Behavioral Finance: It's becoming more evident that investor behavior can have an adverse impact on the results that individual investors achieve, and a significant influence on the mispricing of investment assets. We actively help our clients harness their emotions in order to make better investment decisions. More importantly, new tools that measure investor psychology (with respect to asset classes as well as individual securities) help us identify opportunities and hidden risks in the markets. We believe the investment industry as a whole is just starting to consider how to apply behavioral finance tools to asset management. To help build resilient portfolios, we monitor for pockets of extreme investor psychology and invest contrary to the crowd when we see it.

Tactical Investing: In order to account for ever-changing risk environments, portfolios need to have a tactical element. If volatility and risk levels are constantly changing, shouldn't portfolios include at least some form of adaptability and alternative diversification? Tools such as "relative strength," "tactical beta," technical analysis, and behavior finance have demonstrated their ability to enhance results when combined with fundamental research.

We believe that applying these tools will increase

the resilience of your portfolio: owning assets that benefit from extreme events, using new tools to analyze and manage risk, and maintaining liquidity will help build and maintain a robust portfolio that can weather extreme events and capitalize on opportunities.

Looking into the Future

In recent years, one of the most frequent questions I get from my clients is, "What's your outlook for the future?" When is this economic malaise going to end—is it *ever* going to end? According to the major news networks, or even the average person on the street, the outlook seems bleak. Markets have been substandard for the last twelve to fifteen years. Interest rates are low and are likely to stay that way for some time. The structural fiscal deficit has to be addressed. The Federal Reserve will need to exit its unprecedented monetary policies, and interest rates will eventually rise. The new healthcare laws may make healthcare more expensive. What we've experienced since the start of the

2000s is part of a natural cycle—and there are many advantages to being where we are now, at the tail end of tough times. When the economy is too good for too long, people get what I call "fat, happy, and sloppy." Bad investments are made. Savings and capital are wasted. Businesses become less efficient. Workers become less productive. Opportunities are squandered. These weaknesses build up over time, and inevitably result in a period of transition when the waste must be cleansed from the economy. Like a garden that must be weeded and pruned, the economic landscape will inevitably look ugly for a while during the trimming process. However, this eventually provides the conditions for future growth and ultimately makes way for beauty to be restored. That's where I believe we are right now. Everything has been looking sparse and ugly for a while, but this is all part of the process of renewal—it's what prepares us for the next stage of growth. It's true that our country is facing a number of economic and political challenges. But I believe that the current economic malaise is going to turn around—and it's going to turn around soon. In fact, there are a number of emerging trends that are going to dramatically transform our economy and bring about a renaissance of growth and prosperity.

One trend has to do with economic development in the emerging world. Right now, there are billions of people on the verge of moving into the middle-class. When the average per-capital income in China, for instance, reaches that status, millions of Chinese citizens will go from spending their money primarily on food and shelter to having discretionary income. Citizens in these emerging economies typically save 20 to 30 percent of their earnings. They over-save. Why? Because all they know is being poor and saving for a rainy day. Once it sinks in that they're not poor anymore, their rates of savings will go down and they will begin spending more of their discretionary income. In our globalized world, that means they will be consuming products from all over the world, including products and commodities produced in the United States. As a result of this trend, global trade will become more balanced. Demand will increase, and GDP in the United States will return to higher levels—instead of being under 2 percent, it should go back to 3, 4, and 5 percent. This will be good for markets, and it will be good for investible assets. Interest rates will normalize, and it will actually be profitable for banks to extend loans to small businesses. Those small businesses, in turn, will create new jobs.

Another trend that will help turn around the current cycle is the coming-of-age of the Millennial Generation—the demographic born between 1981 and 2000. Do you remember the economic doldrums of the early 1980s? One of the trends that got us moving out of that down cycle was the baby boomers hitting their mid-thirties. This is the age at which people typically become established in their careers and start families of their own—a process which naturally involves buying houses, purchasing extra cars, buying washing machines and other household necessities. In the mid-1980s, this was a huge engine of economic growth. The oldest members of this generation are going to be entering their mid-thirties within just a couple of years, which is going to create a huge boost for the economy. Once the Millennial Generation hits this stage of life, it's going to spur a similar turnaround in this country—not just economically but politically as well. As this generation moves into established adulthood, they will inevitably become more conservative and pragmatic than they were in their twenties. Young adults who are straight out of college, after all, tend to vote in idealistic and inconsistent ways because they have little real-life experience. But as the Millennials settle into their careers and start having families, they will become more practical. As they participate in society in a more pragmatic fashion, U.S. politics should become more practical as well. We'll see reinvestment in infrastructure, a reduction of the debt, a straightening out of the budget, and fixes for Social Security, Medicare, and Medicaid. This is going to turn the tide both economically and politically in the U.S.—as well as in the developed world as a whole.

There are a number of other trends that promise

to move us into a period of renewed growth. Shale deposits in Utah and Colorado contain three trillion barrels of recoverable oil—that's three times the amount of oil we have used throughout the entirety of human history. Until recently, the cost of extracting this resource from the ground exceeded the price it could be sold for—but as technology develops, that is changing. The International Energy Agency has predicted that the United States will become the world's largest oil producer by 2020. The U.S. is essentially going to become the Middle East of the world within the next ten years; we're going to be exporting oil to the rest of the world, instead of importing it from other countries. This will make the U.S. far more competitive and will change the dynamic of geopolitics. We might not be as hellbent on meddling in the Middle East as we have been in the last seventy years if we no longer needed oil from those countries. Having energy is also a major component to productivity—and having it locally and cheaply will ultimately bring manufacturing back into the country. A lot of people know about these developments, but don't fully understand the dramatic impact they will have on the U.S. economy.

The Next Innovation

Over the past decade there's been plenty of doom and gloom, and predictions for the future are often dismal. But this negative outlook ignores the power of innovation to solve global problems. Sure, the economy has seen tough times over the past few years, and yes, we will face a number of challenges in the years ahead. But this is nothing new: we've gone through these cyclical ups and downs throughout history.

Look at it this way: ever since people were freed to think independently and given the economic liberty to try to make a better life for themselves, the world has been making progress and moving forward. Increasingly, the role of financial advisors is to help our clients see through the fog of short-term thinking and negative projections, and recognize the opportunities for continued progress. Financial advisors of the future will need to become skilled antidotes to the constant news cycle plagued with 24/7 negativism in order to help clients stay focused on the big picture.

Think back to the late 1970s. Then, as now, there was a lot of uncertainty, economic malaise, and a general spirit of anxiety. People were worried about oil shortages, inflation, and unemployment. Folks were getting laid off from manufacturing jobs and our domestic products seemed inferior to other emerging producers around the globe—in fact, a lot of people thought Japan was going to take over the world. At the time, no one could envision what in the world could possibly come along to turn things around.

In 1975, few people knew that Bill Gates was dropping out of Harvard to start a two-man technology company in his garage. The seeds of an entire new industry were being planted—and nobody had a clue as to what they would grow into. In the late '70s—a time when there were no fax machines, no VHS players, no answering machines—who could have imagined the advent of Microsoft and Apple, and the ground-breaking economic boom created by the rise of personal computers?

Necessity creates innovation. And ultimately, innovation is what allows an economy to grow quickly. It's what creates emerging industries and markets that will provide new jobs to replace those that have become obsolete. During recessions, idle individuals (once busy with their old jobs) are forced to become more entrepreneurial and begin focusing on new ideas that would have been squelched under the bureaucracy of their former corporate employers. In light of this, it's no wonder that the '80s and '90s saw the emergence of world-changing technologies like personal computing, the Internet, and mobile telecommunications. In 1979, none of us could have imagined the new industries, jobs, and careers that would replace those that disappeared in the 1970s. The deeper the recession, the deeper the cleansing of the inefficient and outdated modes of business. In my view, the deeper the recession, the more capital is unlocked from less productive uses and made available to new, more productive, and nimbler enterprises.

Everything I understand about emerging industries and technologies indicates that they will prosper in an environment of flexibility, openness, reinvention, and adaptation. I can think of no other society that is more hospitable toward these traits than the United States. Therefore, our economy should benefit as richly as any from the growth of new industries. I believe that the U.S. will play a leading role in the development of the biosciences, nanotechnology, energy, and water resourcing, and that we will see significant growth from these technologies. We should also expect continued leadership and innovation in services that utilize the Internet and "Big Data" to accelerate global economic growth. It is estimated that a tipping point will arrive when the three-billionth person is connected to the global network. This should accelerate the advancement of ideas, breakthroughs, and productivity at a speed that we have never before seen.

It's exciting to think about what kinds of

innovations will emerge in the next several years. The speed of technology—whether through patents, inventions, or productivity growth—is an accelerating trend. An analysis of the history of technology shows that technological change is exponential—the rate of change is speeding up. According to Moore's Law, computer processing speed doubles about every two years. Most likely, the next innovation that revolutionizes our economy will be something as inconceivable as the concepts of personal computers, the Internet, and smart phones were in the '70s. There's no telling what the future holds.

I believe we are in the middle of a transitional phase between the last sustained period of growth (the 1980s and 1990s) and the next sustained period of economic growth (which has probably not yet arrived). In the late 1970s, as now, the future seemed unclear and Americans wondered if our best days were behind us. What we know now is that the next twenty years ushered in a period of American renewal, growth, wealth creation, technology innovation, and an impressive bull market for investors.

We often hear the following: "But this time it is different." Yes, every decade and every generation is different, and while history does not necessarily repeat itself, it certainly does rhyme.

I have always felt that optimism is the only mindset that leads to success. In life, you cannot always control your circumstances, but you can always control your attitude. We are all free to decide to be positive or negative—it's a choice, not a condition forced upon us. Don't get me wrong—I'm just as concerned as everyone else about the problems that still need to be resolved, and how we will resolve them. But ultimately, the solutions will come. You can't dispute natural laws, economic cycles, and the human spirit. You can't fight against the history of progress. I tell my clients all the time that if we can just be careful and manage risk until the next wave of growth takes hold, we're going to be back to a time when investments go up more than they go down. I'm very optimistic about the future and have good reason to be.

I know how fearful you may be about your future. You likely have already sensed a number of the risks and threats that I have pointed out. I also know that there are other things you may be concerned about (the turmoil in the Middle East, the demise of the dollar, the future of America ... the list goes on). I am constantly thinking about these things as well. But no matter what the future holds, we must proactively manage wealth, prepare for uncertainty, and adapt to the changes taking place. Thank you for reading my take on how the world is changing and my suggestions for what you should do about it. Most of all, I encourage you to be optimistic about The Future of Your Wealth!

Disclaimers

planning, education, experience, and compliance record. NABCAP contracts with Rank Premier Advisors to administer its evaluation process. NABCAP's evaluation and ranking program (including the evaluation and validation).

The views expressed herein are those of the author. All opinions are subject to change without notice. Neither the information provided nor any opinion expressed constitutes a solicitation for the purchase or sale of any security. Past performance is no guarantee of future results. The author does not accept any liability whatsoever for any loss or damage arising from any use of this book and its contents. All data and information and opinions expressed herein are subject to change without notice.

This book does not provide individually tailored investment advice. This book contains general information only, does not take account of the specific circumstances of any reader, and should not be relied upon as authoritative or taken in substitution for the exercise of judgment by any recipient. It has been prepared without regard to the individual financial circumstances and objectives of persons who receive it. The strategies and/or investments discussed in this material may not be suitable for all investors. The author recommends that investors independently evaluate particular investments and strategies, and encourages investors to seek the advice of a Financial Advisor and their tax and legal advisors. Under no circumstances should this publication be construed as a solicitation to buy or sell any security or to participate in any trading or investment strategy, nor should this book, or any part of it, form the basis of, or be relied on in connection with, any contract or commitment whatsoever. The appropriateness of a particular investment or strategy will depend on an investor's individual circumstances and objectives. Each reader should consider the appropriateness of any investment decision as it regards to his or her own circumstances, the full range of information available and appropriate professional advice.

The value of, and income from investments may vary because of changes in interest rates or foreign exchange rates, securities prices or market indexes, operational or financial conditions of companies, geopolitical or other factors.

Past performance is not necessarily a guide to future performance. Estimates of future performance are based on assumptions that may not be realized. The information and opinions in the book constitute judgment as of the date of publication, have been compiled and arrived at from sources believed to be reliable and in good faith (but no representation or warranty, express or implied, is made as to their accuracy, completeness or correctness) and are subject to change without notice.

The information provided is based on tax laws currently in effect and is subject to change. There is a possibility that current tax legislation will be amended or repealed in the future. In that case, the outcome of these planning ideas may not be as advantageous. None of the information herein is to be considered tax advice. All ideas are intended to represent tax facts at the time of publication and are subject to change without notice. All ideas must be reviewed by your tax legal and financial advisors based on your individual situation. Tax laws are complex and subject to change. Individuals are encouraged to consult their tax and legal advisors (a) before establishing a retirement plan or account, and (b) regarding any potential tax, ERISA and related consequences of any investments made under such plan or account.

Any Tax information contained in this book is general and not exhaustive by nature. It is not intended or written to be used, and cannot be used, by any taxpayer for the purpose of avoiding U.S. federal tax laws. Pursuant to the rules of professional conduct set forth in Circular 230, as promulgated by the United States Department of the Treasury, nothing contained in this book was intended or written to be used by any taxpayer for the purpose of avoiding penalties that may be imposed on the taxpayer by the Internal Revenue Service and it cannot be used by any taxpayer for such purpose. Federal and State tax laws are complex and constantly changing.

Asset allocation and diversification do not guarantee a profit or protect against a loss.

Bonds are subject to interest rate risk. When interest rates rise, bond prices fall; generally the longer a bond›s maturity, the more sensitive it is to this risk. Bonds may also be subject to call risk, which is the risk that the issuer will redeem the debt at its option, fully or partially, before the scheduled maturity date. The market value of debt instruments may fluctuate, and proceeds from sales prior to maturity may be more or less than the amount originally invested or the maturity value due to changes in market conditions or changes in the credit quality of the issuer. Bonds are subject to the credit risk of the issuer. This is the risk that the issuer might be unable to make interest and/or principal payments on a timely basis. Bonds are also subject to reinvestment risk, which is the risk that principal and/or interest payments from a given investment may be reinvested at a lower interest rate. International bonds are subject to these and other additional risks such as increased risk of default, greater volatility and currency risk.

Equity securities may fluctuate in response to news on companies, industries, market conditions and general economic environment. Companies paying dividends can reduce or cut payouts at any time.

The case studies presented are for educational and illustrative purposes only and do not indicate future performance.

Past performance is no guarantee of future results. Investment results may vary. Any investment strategies, products and services presented are not appropriate for every investor. Individual clients should review with their Financial Advisors the terms and conditions and risks involved with specific products or services. Neither the information provided nor any opinion expressed constitutes a solicitation for the purchase or sale of any security. All of the illustrations throughout the book are hypothetical and not intended to demonstrate the performance of any specific security, product or investment strategy.

For more information, please contact

matt@mattshafer.us

www.ingramcontent.com/pod-product-compliance
Lightning Source LLC
Chambersburg PA
CBHW050528190326
41458CB00045B/6742/J